ALONE
WITH THE LORD

A Guide for a Personal Day of Prayer

Gordon T. Smith

D1452905

REGENT COLLEGE PUBLISHING
Vancouver, British Columbia

Published 2003 by Regent College Publishing
5800 University Boulevard, Vancouver, BC V6T 2E4 Canada
www.regentpublishing.com

National Library of Canada Cataloguing in Publication Data

Smith, Gordon T., 1953-
  Alone with the Lord: a guide for a personal day of prayer / Gordon T. Smith.

  ISBN 1-55361-070-9 (Canada)
  ISBN 1-57383-239-1 (United States)

  1. Prayer—Christianity. I. Title.
BV210.3.S64 2002   248.3'2   C2002-911466-7

CONTENTS

THE DAY WITH THE LORD

A personal day of prayer provides a wonderful opportunity to bring focus and clarity to our lives—particularly in the midst of challenges, opportunities and perplexities—and to renew our joy and peace in Christ. The day of prayer is a gift that enables us to make spiritual and emotional space for an intentional encounter with Christ, through which we awaken the presence of the Spirit in our lives.

As we remove ourselves from our normal routines and schedules and choose to be alone with the Lord, his Spirit will renew our focus and energy and bring perspective to our life circumstances.

THE GRACE WE SEEK

A day of prayer is an opportunity to intentionally seek the grace of Christ so that we can know, love and serve him. For some, the primary benefit of a day alone with the Lord will be the opportunity to enter into the *school of prayer*, a practice that deepens our experience of Christ by fostering our capacity for intimacy with him. Because the natural bent of our hearts and minds is isolation and autonomy, we need the day of prayer to cultivate our capacity for intimacy. And this, more than anything else, makes the day worthwhile. What we find is that our *daily* prayers are renewed and animated by the experience of an entire day in prayer.

Or we may come to the day of prayer with a key decision on the table. In this circumstance, we are seeking the mind of Christ for a decision we need to make—a choice that will determine a key direction for our lives. When we are facing a critical choice, the grace we seek in a day of prayer is to know the guiding witness of the Spirit that enables us to see our circumstances clearly and respond with courage and wisdom to the call and guidance of God. Seeking to know, love and serve Jesus, we come to the day of prayer longing to know specifically how this will find expression in light of the decision we are facing. Surely the critical choices of our lives—whether to stay with our current job or respond to another opportunity, how to respond to a significant moral or ethical dilemma, whether to remain single or to marry, indeed any number of decisions and choices that we are regularly called upon to make—merit extended time alone with God. These choices affect our lives and inevitably shape the lives of others whom we love and serve as well; as such they are decisions that require that we take the time to slow down, step aside from the normal routine of life and work, and make the time to be alone with the Lord.

Even if our primary longing when we come to the day of prayer is the grace to choose well, the day will always be a school of prayer—an opportunity to foster and cultivate intimacy with Christ. The grace to see our circumstances clearly and the renewed courage to do what we are being called to do will arise out of our deepened experience with Christ. Thus the first objective is always to know Christ and grow in our capacity to love and serve him. We never come to the day merely to get a "word from the Lord." To do so would be to "use" the Lord as nothing but a kind of fortuneteller whom we ask to respond to a dilemma we are facing.

Therefore, instead of forcing the issue or pressing prematurely for a resolution to the question that occasioned the day of prayer, we must let the longing for clarity or direction emerge in the course of the day. By seeking the face of Christ first, we often discover that our longing for guidance is fulfilled by the end of the day. God knows what we need and will grant us the peace to do what he is calling us to do.

The plan that follows focuses on seeking the grace of Christ:

1. To experience with assurance the love of God;

2. To experience the convicting and liberating ministry of the Spirit;

3. To experience the illuminating power of truth;

4. To experience the Spirit's personal guidance in the face of a critical decision.

These are four distinct dimensions of the Spirit's ministry to the Christian, which cultivate our capacity to know, love and serve Jesus.

ORDERING THE DAY

It is usually best to approach a day of prayer with an order to the day; this does not diminish spontaneity or the free work of the Spirit, but is rather an expression of intentionality. There are both theological and practical reasons for coming to a day of prayer with such a plan. Theologically, we come wanting to meet the risen Christ, and so we need an order that is oriented specifically to the Lord Jesus Christ. To foster this longing, we are wise to use an approach that has historical precedence in the history of the church and an order congruent with the character of the self-revelation of Christ in Scripture.[1]

Practically, our ordered intentionally keeps us focused on Christ. It is all too easy for a day of prayer to become an extended time of personal solitude and nothing more. Though we all require times of solitude, a day of prayer is specifically a day *with* the Lord. Because our minds easily wander and our hearts are prone to self-indulgence, a guide to our day of prayer keeps us alert

1. The Plan for this self-guided day of prayer is adapted from *The Spiritual Exercises* of Ignatius of Loyola.

and focused on our desire to cultivate our capacity to know, love and serve Jesus.

While there are a number of ways in which we could order our day, this approach will divide the day into four central or primary sessions that correspond to the four ways in which we seek the grace of Christ. These sessions will be framed by a time of preparation at the beginning of the day and a concluding session of benediction at the end of the day.

Following is a potential time guide for your prayers. These times are merely a suggestion, and you should adjust these segments for prayer in a manner congruent your own needs.

8:00 a.m.	Prelude: Beginning well
8:30	Session #1
10:00	Break
10:30	Session #2
12:00	Break
1:00 p.m.	Session #3
2:30	Break
3:00	Session #4
4:30	Postlude: Conclusion and Benediction
5:00	Go in peace

As discussed previously, this order for the day centers on *four* extended sessions that correspond to the four dimensions of God's grace that we seek. Each extended session of focused prayer is also designed to build on the grace experienced in the previous session.

Each of the four major sessions follows a similar internal order, where you will:

• Identify the grace to be sought and, through a prayer of intercession, ask God for this grace and to prepare your heart to receive it.

• Consider a psalm that highlights this grace; as you identify with the psalm, you cultivate your capacity to accept this grace.

• Practice the assigned spiritual exercise that arises out of the psalm; this will enable you to know the grace for the "hour."

• Enter the discipline of silence.

• Write a journal entry, expressing your experience of prayer in this session. (Space has been provided at the end of this booklet.)

A NOTE ON THE CENTRAL PLACE OF THE PSALMS

For a day of prayer there are few resources as significant as the Old Testament Psalms. These are the prayers of the church, the people of God, so it makes sense for them to inform our prayers.

For each segment of the day, an appropriate psalm has been selected for meditation in order to focus our attention on the grace we are seeking during that session.

It is helpful to approach each psalm with the following plan:

• Identify the spiritual longing or emotional aspiration of the psalm, which corresponds to the grace you seek in that hour of prayer.

• Identify the foundational truth or doctrinal principle that will enable this longing or aspiration to be fulfilled.

• Identify the spiritual exercise by which you can live in the light of this truth and so experience the fulfillment of this longing or aspiration.

A PLACE FOR SILENCE

Before beginning the day of prayer, it is also important to highlight the vital place that silence will have in this day alone with the Lord.

As Deitrich Bonhoeffer notes in his spiritual classic *Life Together*, a day alone with the Lord enables us to live with integrity in community.[2] Bonhoeffer goes on to insist that the key ingredient of solitude is *silence*. While readings, guided prayers and exercises for a day of prayer are outlined in the following pages, the central mark of the day will be silence. For it is in silence that we meet and hear Christ and attend to the inner witness of his Spirit through the Word of God—not only the *inscripturated* Word in the Bible, but also the specific Word of God speaking into the particular circumstances of our lives. To hear this Word, we need to be still, so silence will be the anchor and central feature of our time alone with the Lord.

This guide to prayer suggests spending 15–20 minutes in silence as part of each segment of the day. Remain in

2. Dietrich Bonhoeffer, *Life Together*, trans. Daniel W. Bloesch (Minneapolis: Fortress Press, 1996; first published in German, 1939), 83.

this silence. When distracted, gently bring your thoughts back to the focus of the hour. Avoid the temptation to get up and walk around or to read what is at hand. Be still even when it does not seem, at least immediately, to be worthwhile. In time you will find that silence bears fruit—God is in the silence and speaks in silence. And as you learn to be still, you will cultivate the capacity to know and hear the One who loves you.

To foster this solitude, find a quiet church sanctuary, retreat center or someplace where you will not be distracted or interrupted. Leave the cellular phone and the pager at home, letting yourself be disconnected and out of touch (knowing that this day alone will actually enable you to be truly in "touch" when you return to your regular duties and responsibilities). As a parent, find someone to take care of the children for the day (and perhaps even offer them the same gift in return).

Even in the most still and quiet setting, it is easy to be distracted. There are noises in the distance—the play of a child or the passing of a truck—and the noises of others—the shuffling feet or cough of a fellow retreatant. And there are the noises of our own thoughts—the worries and temptations that distract us from prayer, sometimes unwittingly. Whether the noise is external or internal, try not to be irritated or frustrated by these distractions. Instead, seek to intentionally quiet your heart and mind by gently turning from the noises around you and in your heart, making a conscious and deliberate choice to be still before the Lord, your Maker and Redeemer.

Beginning Well

Suggested time: 8:00 a.m.

To enter into the day with an overview of the grace you are seeking for this day, read Isaiah 55 (see text below). The structure of this chapter of Scripture corresponds to the structure of the day of prayer. As you read, be conscious of the way the Spirit is drawing you into this day alone with Christ.

Read the passage a second time, being attentive to each phrase.

Make notes in your journal as you read. What stands out to you from this text of Scripture and impresses itself on your mind?

ISAIAH 55 (NRSV)

THE CALL TO LISTEN (VERSES 1–3A)

Ho, everyone who thirsts, come to the waters; and you that have no money, come, buy and eat! Come,

buy wine and milk without money and without price.
Why do you spend your money for that which is not
bread, and your labor for that which does not satisfy?
Listen carefully to me, and eat what is good, and
delight yourselves in rich food. Incline your ear, and
come to me; listen, so that you may live.

THE ASSURANCE OF GOD'S LOVE (VERSES 3B–5)

I will make with you an everlasting covenant, my
steadfast, sure love for David. See, I made him a wit-
ness to the peoples, a leader and commander for the
peoples. See, you shall call nations that you do not
know, and nations that do not know you shall run to
you, because of the LORD your God, the Holy One of
Israel, for he has glorified you.

THE CALL TO REPENTANCE AND THE CONFIDENCE OF GOD'S FORGIVENESS (VERSES 6–7)

Seek the LORD while he may be found, call upon him
while he is near; let the wicked forsake their way, and
the unrighteous their thoughts; let them return to the
LORD, that he may have mercy on them, and to our
God, for he will abundantly pardon.

THE CALL TO LIVE IN THE TRUTH, CONFIDENT OF ITS REDEMPTIVE POWER (VERSES 8–11)

For my thoughts are not your thoughts, nor are your ways my ways, says the LORD. For as the heavens are higher than the earth, so are my ways higher than your ways and my thoughts than your thoughts. For as the rain and the snow come down from heaven, and do not return there until they have watered the earth, making it bring forth and sprout, giving seed to the sower and bread to the eater, so shall my word be that goes out from my mouth; it shall not return to me empty, but it shall accomplish that which I purpose, and succeed in the thing for which I sent it.

THE CALL TO LIVE IN JOY AND RECEIVE GOD'S GUIDANCE IN PEACE (VERSES 12–13)

For you shall go out in joy, and be led back in peace; the mountains and the hills before you shall burst into song, and all the trees of the field shall clap their hands. Instead of the thorn shall come up the cypress; instead of the brier shall come up the myrtle; and it shall be to the LORD for a memorial, for an everlasting sign that shall not be cut off.

After reading Isaiah 55, identify what you anticipate will be the central or defining element of the day for you. Are you seeking the grace to know that you are loved, the convicting ministry of the Spirit or the illuminating power of truth? Or are you seeking the grace to go out with peace and joy, confident in God's guidance in the midst of a critical choice? Reading Isaiah 55 can serve to highlight your longings as you come to this day, particularly if there is one dimension of God's grace that really stands out to you.

Once you identify this defining element of your day alone with Christ, you do not need to rush the time or seek this grace immediately. You can approach the day in a fashion that is consistent with the pace of God's work in your heart, confident that this grace will come. You can give the day over to God, letting go of the need to control the day in order to arrive at a particular conclusion. You can enter into each phase of the day confident that God knows the longing of your heart.

THE GRACE TO EXPERIENCE THAT WE ARE LOVED

Suggested time: 8:30–10:00 a.m.

The spiritual life rests on only one possible foundation: the assurance that we are loved, the confidence that God accepts us and cares for us. We begin our day of prayer here with a re-affirmation and a renewed awareness of this love. Everything else in the spiritual life—and every other part of the day of prayer—flows out of this confidence in the assurance of God's love.

1. CENTER THOUGHTS

"Lord, in your goodness and mercy, grant me the grace that I seek—and, as I begin this day with you, I long for this: to know your love, to experience your love and to live my life out of this confidence."

In Ephesians 3:17, Paul identifies this grace as being "rooted and grounded in love." Note how this grace is situated in the prayer of Paul in Ephesians 3:14–19:

> *For this reason I bow my knees before the Father, from whom every family in heaven and on earth takes its name. I pray that, according to the riches of his glory, he may grant that you may be strengthened in your inner being with power through his Spirit, and that Christ may dwell in your hearts through faith, as you are being rooted and grounded in love. I pray that you may have the power to comprehend, with all the saints, what is the breadth and length and height and depth, and to know the love of Christ that surpasses knowledge, so that you may be filled with all the fullness of God.*

For some, this grace will come easily. For others, perhaps because of family of origin issues or the unique challenge of their immediate circumstances, this grace will come more slowly. We seek, to the extent that we are able at this time in our lives and for this day, a deep, heart-felt assurance that God knows and loves us personally and specifically and calls us by name.

2. CONSIDER PSALM 100

> *Make a joyful noise to the LORD, all the earth.*
> *Worship the LORD with gladness;*
> *come into his presence with singing.*

Know that the LORD is God.
It is he that made us, and we are his;
we are his people, and the sheep of his pasture.

Enter his gates with thanksgiving,
and his courts with praise.
Give thanks to him, bless his name.

For the LORD is good;
his steadfast love endures forever,
and his faithfulness to all generations.

In this session, we long to know the love of God. Psalm 100 reminds us that God's love endures forever and declares that God is good, that he is faithful to all generations. As we consider this doctrinal truth, we can be confident that God will fulfill our longing to know his love, and we can find joy in this assurance.

Psalm 100 also reminds us of the most fundamental discipline of the spiritual life: *thanksgiving*. (We enter his "gates" through the act of giving thanks for his goodness.) It is through thanksgiving that we lift up our hearts to the Lord and enter into his presence ("his gates").

Read the psalm a second time and prepare to enter into the spiritual practice of thanksgiving.

3. SPIRITUAL DISCIPLINE: THANKSGIVING

The spiritual practice or discipline that enables us to

know with assurance that we are loved is thanksgiving.

For this exercise, give thanks by enumerating the signs, or indicators, of God's goodness. It is most fruitful to be specific, identifying the particular ways that God has been good to you.

The following exercise may help you approach the practice of thanksgiving:

• Identify ten things for which you are grateful—ten indicators of God's goodness to you. Rather than listing attributes of God's goodness in the vague or general sense, consider specifically how God has been good to you. List these indicators in your journal.

• After a few moments of silence, identity ten more things for which to give thanks. How has God been faithful to you in the last few days or weeks?

• After another 3–5 minutes of silence, identify ten more things for which you are thankful.

4. SILENCE

Dwell in the conscious awareness of God's goodness for 15–20 minutes.

5. JOURNAL ENTRY

Now take a few minutes to write about what stands out from your prayer—particularly in the silence. Comment on your experience of prayer—has God impressed anything upon you? You may find it fruitful to address your journal directly to the Lord—as a written response to his presence and Word to you on this day.

SESSION #2

THE GRACE TO EXPERIENCE THE CONVICTING AND LIBERATING MINISTRY OF THE SPIRIT

Suggested Time: 10:30 a.m.–12:00 noon

The encounter with God necessarily means that we come face to face with ourselves, and this includes an awareness of how we have failed God "in thought, word and deed, by what we have done and by what we have left undone," to quote the line from the classic liturgical prayers of confession. So our day includes the simple act of seeking to respond with heart and mind to the convicting ministry of the Spirit.

1. CENTER THOUGHTS

"O Spirit of Christ, as I turn from any form of burdensome false guilt, grant me this grace: to know your convicting ministry that will lead to freedom and strength."

As we long for the grace to experience the convicting ministry of the Spirit, the Spirit will not condemn us, but will lead us to freedom, so it is essential that we are alert to any experience of false guilt—a burdensome and crippling guilt that does not come from God.

We may feel guilt in the face of wrongs that we have already confessed. But since God is one who forgives, we can be assured that this guilt is not from God, and we can ask God to help us accept his forgiveness again.

We may also feel guilty when we are burdened by the expectations of others or when we fail to live up to our own expectations. This is burdensome and useless—or false—guilt. As we acknowledge false guilt, the liberating and convicting call of the Spirit emerges so that we can walk in freedom. Jesus speaks of the Spirit as one who will convict the world of sin (John 16:8). Psalm 139:23–24 expresses the work of the Spirit in this way:

> *Search me, O God, and know my heart;*
> *test me and know my thoughts.*
> *See if there is any wicked way in me,*
> *and lead me in the way everlasting.*

2. CONSIDER PSALM 32

> *Happy are those whose transgression is forgiven,*
> *   whose sin is covered.*
> *Happy are those to whom the LORD imputes no*
> *iniquity,*

and in whose spirit there is no deceit.

While I kept silence, my body wasted away
* through my groaning all day long.*
For day and night your hand was heavy upon
me;
my strength was dried up as by the heat of
* summer.*

Then I acknowledged my sin to you,
* and I did not hide my iniquity;*
I said, "I will confess my transgressions to the
* LORD,"*
and you forgave the guilt of my sin.

Therefore let all who are faithful offer prayer to
you;
at a time of distress, the rush of mighty waters
shall not reach them.
You are a hiding place for me; you preserve me
from trouble;
you surround me with glad cries of deliverance.

I will instruct you and teach you the way you
* should go;*
I will counsel you with my eye upon you.
Do not be like a horse or a mule, without
understanding,
whose temper must be curbed with bit and

bridle,
else it will not stay near you.

Many are the torments of the wicked,
but steadfast love surrounds those who trust in
the LORD.
Be glad in the LORD and rejoice, O righteous,
and shout for joy, all you upright in heart.

In this hour, we long to know the convicting and liberating ministry of the Holy Spirit. To receive this ministry, we have to know God's forgiveness.

As Psalm 32 reveals, God is one who forgives our sin, so we can approach him in confidence as the Spirit convicts us. The psalm also demonstrates the spiritual practice that enables us to live in this confidence: the discipline of *confession* (also known as the *examination of conscience*).

Read the psalm a second time and prepare to enter into the spiritual practice of confession.

3. SPIRITUAL DISCIPLINE: CONFESSION

The spiritual discipline that enables us to know the convicting ministry of the Spirit is confession. Confession involves several distinct acts:

• We acknowledge our wrong—that what we have said or done is inconsistent with the character and will of God.

• We accept that we are responsible, and that we

cannot blame others or claim extenuating circumstances.
- We humbly ask for mercy: "Christ have mercy."
- We confidently receive the forgiveness of God.

With a quiet heart and open hands, consider how the Spirit may be convicting you. Earnestly ask for mercy without making excuses. Then accept God's forgiveness.

4. SILENCE

Dwell in the conscious awareness of God's mercy and forgiveness for 15–20 minutes.

5. JOURNAL ENTRY

In your journal, write about your prayers in this hour. Where have you experienced the convicting ministry of the Spirit? Did you also experience any false guilt? Address your journal to the Lord, responding to your experience of his mercy and liberating forgiveness on this day.

THE GRACE TO EXPERIENCE THE ILLUMINATING POWER OF TRUTH

Suggested time: 1:00–2:30 p.m.

We live in freedom when we live in the truth, and we are transformed by the renewal of our minds. The Spirit renews and transforms us as we engage the truth with heart and mind, particularly the truth revealed through Holy Scripture.

1. CENTER THOUGHTS

"Lord, grant me this grace—to know the truth that can set me free, the grace of a heart and mind that is permeated with your Word."

The grace we seek for this hour is captured by the words of Colossians 3:15–16:

And let the peace of Christ rule in your hearts, to which indeed you were called in the one body. And be thankful. Let the word of Christ dwell in you richly;

teach and admonish one another in all wisdom; and
with gratitude in your hearts sing psalms, hymns, and
spiritual songs to God.

We long for the Word of Christ to dwell in us richly, but this will only be the case if the peace of Christ rules in our hearts, so we need to cultivate a meekness of heart and a posture of joyful receptivity to the Word of God (see also 1 Thessalonians 1:6 and James 1:18–21).

2. CONSIDER PSALM 119:1–16

Happy are those whose way is blameless,
who walk in the law of the LORD.
Happy are those who keep his decrees,
who seek him with their whole heart,
who also do no wrong, but walk in his ways.

You have commanded your precepts
to be kept diligently.
O that my ways may be steadfast
in keeping your statutes!
Then I shall not be put to shame,
having my eyes fixed on all your commandments.

I will praise you with an upright heart,
when I learn your righteous ordinances.
I will observe your statutes;
do not utterly forsake me.

How can young people keep their way pure?
By guarding it according to your word.

With my whole heart I seek you;
do not let me stray from your commandments.
I treasure your word in my heart,
so that I may not sin against you.

Blessed are you, O LORD;
teach me your statutes.
With my lips I declare
all the ordinances of your mouth.
I delight in the way of your decrees
as much as in all riches.

I will meditate on your precepts,
and fix my eyes on your ways.
I will delight in your statutes;
I will not forget your word.

In this hour, we long to know the joy of living in the truth. Psalm 119 reminds us that God is our teacher, so we can confidently ask him to lead us to his truth. This psalm also calls us to the spiritual practice of meditation in order to live in the reality that God is our teacher.

Read the psalm a second time and prepare to enter into the spiritual discipline of meditation.

3. SPIRITUAL DISCIPLINE: MEDITATION

The spiritual practice that enables us to experience the illuminating power of truth is *meditation*. When we *meditate* on Scripture, we read in a manner that allows God to speak to us through the ancient text. In so doing, it is vital that we respect and honor the character of the Bible. This is the Word of God, and we attend to this Word, recognizing that in reading we feed our souls and sustain our lives.

However, this is also a human text—letters and oracles, psalms and narratives. While written through the inspiration of the Spirit, the Bible is a very human document written by real people. This reality does not diminish the text for us but reminds us that just as the incarnation was the very means by which God is known through Christ Jesus, the human character of the Bible is the actual means by which God reveals his divine Word to us. So we hear the Word of God as we attend to these human texts and read poetry as poetry, narrative as narrative, letter as letter, and history as history.

While our meditation is on the text, we yearn to know Christ through the text. To this end, we need to listen with heart and mind as we meditate. Though we engage our intellect and seek understanding, we also read with an open and meek heart, eagerly seeking to receive the Word of God with joy—as Paul tells his readers in 1 Thessalonians 1, a joy "inspired by the Holy Spirit."

Below you will find a list of texts on which you might

30

meditate during this segment of the day of prayer. Rather than reading all of them, choose one and read it carefully and intentionally. As you consider the options for this reading, ask the Spirit to draw your attention to one of them.

Read the text slowly, considering the cadence of the passage and its flow or presentation, while also being attentive to your own emotional response.

Consider the following questions as you read: What stands out for you in the text? What strikes you personally—not as truth that others need to know, but as truth that is pertinent to your own circumstances, calling and relationships? This distinction is important, for the purpose of the day of prayer is not to hear God's word for others, but to hear God's specific word to your personal situation, circumstances and need. Avoid the temptation to see how this text might help others or serve as the basis for a sermon or a Bible study. During this hour, we seek to open *our* hearts to the Spirit's illumination of our minds.

Meditation: Choose one of the following three texts:

• *Read the Epistle of Paul to the Philippians*—Read it through twice. On the second reading, note what impresses you, with particular attention to the principles that shape the Christian life. This is a good choice if you have plenty of time to read and reflect. What you seek is a deep awareness and appreciation for the character of the Christian life—its focus, its contours and its internal dynamic. As you read, consider how God is calling you to live in the grace of the Lord Jesus Christ (note the benediction in Philippians 4:23).

• *Read Chapter 40:1–11 and Chapter 58 from the prophet Isaiah*—Be attentive to the way in which the texts reveal the character of God—both his mercy and gracious manner as well as his firm and specific call to live with Christian integrity. Then read Chapter 40:1–11 a second time.

• *Read two accounts of Jesus as he encounters others* (Luke 8:22–25 and Luke 8:40–48)—In each case, the focus is Jesus—what he says, what he does and what it means for you. Seek specifically a personal encounter with the Christ who is revealed through these texts.

4. SILENCE

In an extended time of silence (at least 15–20 minutes), dwell in the truth that has been impressed upon you during your reading and meditation.

Focus your thoughts on what you recognize as the Word of God to you in this hour. Be confident that as you sit in silence, God will draw your attention to what he would have you know and experience.

5. JOURNAL ENTRY

Write in your journal about what has emerged through your time of meditation, prayer and silence. What is God's Word to you through the text on which you have been meditating?

The Grace to Experience Guidance for a Critical and Important Choice

Suggested time: 3:00–4:30 p.m.

As mentioned at the beginning, you may be coming to this day of prayer precisely because you seek guidance in the face of a critical choice. However, even if no decision is pressing, and you came to the day to experience a school of prayer and to nurture intimacy with Christ, the day alone with the Lord is always an opportunity to hear God's call into the specific challenges and opportunities of your life and work.

As we come to the conclusion of the day, we are conscious that we are being called back into the world. With this fourth prayer session, we anticipate our return to the daily duties and relationships of our lives. We move from retreat to re-engagement. What we seek is the grace to live in the world in a manner that consciously arises out of our prayers. If we are making a critical

33

decision, we long that this choice would be informed by our prayers and by our encounter with Christ. Our prayers and time alone with the Lord are not a means to escape from the world but an experience that enables us to live with integrity and grace in the world.

1. CENTER THOUGHTS

"Lord grant me the grace to choose well—to engage my world with the peace that you give me, to have courage in the face of difficulty and confidence that you are guiding me."

We seek to know the peace of God for a choice that is before us—that, in the words of Isaiah 55, we would "go out with joy and be led back in peace." This grace is highlighted by the words of Philippians 4:7:

And the peace of God, which surpasses all understanding, will guard your hearts and your minds in Christ Jesus.

2. CONSIDER PSALM 23

The LORD is my shepherd, I shall not want.
He makes me lie down in green pastures;
he leads me beside still waters;
he restores my soul.
He leads me in right paths for his name's sake.

Even though I walk through the darkest valley,
I fear no evil; for you are with me;
your rod and your staff—they comfort me.

You prepare a table before me in the presence of
my enemies;
you anoint my head with oil;
my cup overflows.

Surely goodness and mercy shall follow me all
the days of my life,
and I shall dwell in the house of the LORD my
whole life long.

In this hour, we yearn for God's personal care and guidance. As Psalm 23 reminds us of God's providential care and goodness, we can seek God's guidance confidently.

In order to walk with confidence—a lack of anxiety or fear—in the assurance of God's guidance, we need to *discern* God's peace. Read Psalm 23 a second time and prepare to enter into the spiritual practice of discernment.

3. SPIRITUAL DISCIPLINE: DISCERNMENT

The spiritual discipline that enables us to respond to the particular call of God and know his guidance in the midst of a choice or critical decision is *discernment*.

As we face the critical choice ahead of us, we need to

consider how we sense God's peace. We can only attend to this peace if we are alert to the presence of desolation in our hearts. Any hint we have of fear, anger, discouragement or desolation should cause us to reconsider and reflect again. God only leads in peace.[3]

But just because we have peace does not mean that we now know the mind of God. During the course of the day, particularly now as we come to its conclusion, we may have a sense of what God is calling us to do. We may think we have peace concerning a potential course of action. But this peace must be tested; we need to know if the peace actually comes from God.

To discern this, we must ask ourselves three questions, which reflect the classic temptations that Jesus faced in the wilderness:

• Is there anything in this peace that arises from an inordinate desire for wealth or financial security?

• Is there anything in this peace that arises from an inordinate desire for power or influence?

• Is there anything in this peace that arises from an inordinate longing for recognition or affirmation?

If we can say that we long for and seek nothing but God's good and perfect will (Romans 12:2), then we can discern that we feel God's peace. If we are able to say that what we seek reflects the "true…honorable…just…and

3. For a more complete explanation of why we must not choose in desolation but rather choose only in peace—a peace that is "tested"— consider reading Gordon T. Smith, *Listening to God in Times of Choice* (InterVarsity Press, 1997).

pure…" (Philippians 4:8), then we can rest in God's peace for that decision.

4. SILENCE

In 15–20 minutes of silence, attend to the presence of Christ and allow his Spirit to confirm the peace that you are experiencing—or to challenge that peace through a demonstration of misguided motives or aspirations. Of course, our motives are never "pure," but we should be able to say that what ultimately shapes our actions is not so much our misguided motives as the peace of Christ.

5. JOURNAL ENTRY

In response to God's guidance, record in your journal what you are feeling about the choice or decision you need to make.

POSTLUDE:

CONCLUSION AND BENEDICTION

Suggested time: 4:30 p.m.

As you conclude, read through your journal entries for each segment of the day, including the opening prelude. Be attentive to recurring themes. Note connections between the entries, particularly to the way in which journal entries may have new meaning in light of earlier or later entries.

Consider what from this day needs to be shared with:

• A spiritual director, spiritual friend, pastor or accountability group;

• Those with whom you live (either a spouse or housemate);

• Those who are affected by what might arise from this day.

As you prepare to re-engage with the world, receive this benediction from Numbers 6:24–26:

The LORD bless you and keep you;
the LORD make his face to shine upon you,
    and be gracious to you;
the LORD lift up his countenance upon you,
    and give you peace.

AMEN.

NOTES

ALONE WITH THE LORD

NOTES

ALONE WITH THE LORD

NOTES

ALONE WITH THE LORD

NOTES

CPSIA information can be obtained
at www.ICGtesting.com
Printed in the USA
LVOW03s0136271217

560785LV00001B/40/P

9 781573 832397